Digital Danger

If You Think Your Kid is Safe Online, Think Again!

ISBN-13: 978-1481896979
ISBN-10: 1481896970
Cover Design by Kenn Schroder

Contents

Acknowledgements

We wish to thank all educators and law enforcement professionals who work to create a safe environment and bright future for our youth. People in these career fields often toil without the rewards that accompany other careers. We know that the better that you do your job, the less likely you are to be noticed, or thanked.

No body of work is ever created without building upon the experiences, theories, research and perspective of others. We would like to thank those who have shared their knowledge with us.

Tim would like to acknowledge the contribution of his mentor, Dr Joseph Quaranta who inspired him to stretch in the pursuit of scholarship.

This book would not have been possible without the design expertise and coaching support of Kenn Schroder, the editing support of M.Todd Smith, and Tim's caring wife Katey who encourages and supports his pursuit of new endeavors.

Don would like to thank the parents, school staff, and students who helped improve his understanding of these issues over the last 15 years. In addition, Don would like to thank the board members of The Digital Innocence Recovery Group whose collective experience has provided a depth of knowledge to draw upon.

About Us

Officer Don Stanko

Don Stanko has been a Law Enforcement Officer for over 20 years. Don has served as a D.A.R.E. Officer, Community Relations Officer, Crime Prevention Officer and Safety Town Director. Trained to investigate Internet related crimes; he specializes in bullying and cyberbullying prevention. Noticing an increase in computer related crimes, Don co-established the non-profit organization Digital Innocence Recovery Group to help students, teachers, and parents prevent bullying, cyber bullying and other computer - related crimes.

Dr. Tim Conrad

A 30-year education veteran, Tim has served as a teacher, counselor, coach, and counselor educator teaching students from kindergarten through graduate school. A frequent speaker at the state and national level he is passionate about helping educators and parents "get in the way" of negative influences that harm those they care about. He is the founder of Resilient Resources LLC; a consulting firm that specializes in helping others manage change by maximizing potential. He is also the author of Retire Happy: How to Remain Relevant, Reputable and Resilient.

Our Purpose

Digital Danger is a non-profit organization dedicated to the prevention of Internet related crime. The Digital Innocence logo is a shield. A shield is strong to keeps thing that could harm us away. We instinctively place shields in front of those we hold most dear, those areas where we are most vulnerable. You get the idea: the outside of the shield deflects danger; the inside of the shield protects those areas where we care about. We spend a lot of time trying to keep our kids safe. We talk to them about stranger danger, make sure that they try hard in school, get enough sleep, eat a healthy diet, monitor their friends, and keep them away from drugs and alcohol. These are common shields we use to protect our kids. Our intention is to equip you with another shield that will deflect the digital danger that threatens you and the children in your life. We wrote this guide for anyone who cares about kids and want to keep these kids safe in the digital world. Parents, teachers, counselors, law enforcement professionals, media specialists, librarians, grandparents, aunts, uncles have found our practical suggestions helpful.

Introduction

Paradigm Shifts

Co-author and Police Officer Don can still hear his mentor's words; "I've never known a child to get into trouble from the safety of his own bedroom." His hope was that we could dispense these words of wisdom to parents of delinquent children. At the time, the statement made a lot of sense, but that was 1991. Times change and along the way Don began to notice that his mentor's advice did not keep all danger at bay.

Fast forward to January 1997. Don just accepted a position as the police division's crime prevention officer and felt confident that the last five and a half years sufficiently prepared him for any problem the public might encounter. His confidence waned three days later, when a parent called to warn him about the newest danger faced by children. A caller recounted that two girls had maliciously bullied her daughter. Recalling his academy days and the advice of his mentor, Don suggested that the girl distance herself from the girls and spend some quality time at home, where the bullies couldn't taunt her.

He was quite pleased with himself until the resident said, "She was at home when this happened! It happened on the Internet." This encounter resulted in a major paradigm shift for young police officer Don. Bullies found a new weapon, the Internet. Home is no longer a safe refuge from bullies.

Co-author Tim's first experience with cyberbullying occurred during roughly the same time period. A student came into his school counseling office complaining that another student was bullying her. Tim began documenting what the bully said. The student stated: "No need to do that." She handed Tim a printout of the bullying conversation from her AOL account.

That was a game changer. Since then we've felt that parents, schools, and law enforcement have been playing catch up to the dangers that technology presents. If you're a student, parent, teacher, or police officer, you've faced the challenge of applying what we know about safety in the "real" world and adapting it to our lives in the digital world. This book provides you with the depth of 30 years of combined experience along with hard learned lessons from hundreds of parents and educators. Hopefully, this book will give you a strong foundation, upon which you can build a proficient understanding of the "Digital World".

One of the main lessons that we hope you take from this book is that although technology has revolutionized the world, you do not have to have a lot of tech savvy to keep you and your family safe online.

Chapter One
Current Trends in Digital Technology and Social Media

Kids and Technology

Today, our children live in a *Dual World Reality*. There is the "Real World" and a "Digital World". With improving technology and the ubiquitous nature of the Internet, the "Digital World" is becoming a more essential part of our lives. This comes with some complications. Even though our children are considered "Digital Natives", they still need to develop a better understanding of virtual social interaction. Most students experience asynchronous development when it comes to understanding online social interactions.

Specifically, they are more adept at reading social interactions in the "Real World"; than in the "Digital World" where they are much less proficient.

Let's first consider how we experience both worlds. In the "Real World", we experience things in the first person. This means we are fully engaged in the moment. In the "Digital World", we experience things with a third person perspective. The difference would be akin to listening to a story instead of being directly involved in the action. This makes us feel somewhat removed from what is taking place.

To further complicate matters, in the "Real World" there are immediate consequences for our actions. While in the "Digital World", people are more likely to experience a delay in consequences for their actions. What you type or the things you do to other people in the "Digital World" may not affect you for days, months or even years later. Take, for example, a child who creates a rumor or types something cruel about another student. The child who wrote the statement might not experience the consequences of what they wrote until they attend school the following day, if at all.

In fact, many victims of rumors have a hard time confronting the individual who started the rumor, if they can ascertain the origins of the rumor in the first place. In the "Digital World", this Third Person perspective and the delay of consequences diminishes our ability to accurately interpret both risk and consequence.

Being on the Internet makes us feel safer and more secure; that feeling can get us in a lot of trouble. Consider for a moment, where the "fight or flight" response comes from. This is one of the most primitive responses your brain creates, one that is triggered by the recognition of danger.

Unfortunately, the delay in consequences for online actions can prevent us from accurately assessing "Digital World" dangers. Combine that with being in an environment considered safe, like a child's bedroom, and your son or daughter could experience a heightened, but inaccurate perception of safety and security.

Accurate risk assessment is not the only obstacle your child may face when venturing into the "Digital World". Both authors have encountered many issues involving communication barriers and ethical judgment.

Let's first consider online communication. Communicating in the "Digital World" through email or text messaging is fine for conveying simple messages, like "I will meet you at the Mall @ 5:00 pm" or "What was the homework for Geometry today?"

However, children have adopted email and text messages for much more sophisticated interactions, like resolving a disagreement or debating a point of view. This complicates the communication process especially when it involves uncomfortable topics.

Whenever Officer Don talks to a high school or middle school, he often asks the question "How many of you have either tried to resolve a disagreement experience a breakup through email or text message?" The response is always the same; well over half to three quarters of the students raise their hands. Then, Don follows up with another question, "How does that work out for you?" The response is always the same, wide spread laughter! During focus groups, students will often share accounts of escalating arguments, where a simple discussion deteriorates rapidly during a text chat. One student commented "Really, if I said it in person, it would have never gotten this bad." Despite the low success rate of text message debates, texting about an uncomfortable topic may seem less intimidating than a live discussion. For this reason, many students opt to use texting instead of engaging in a face – to - face confrontation.

Communicating in the "Digital World" has its risks, mainly because it differs so much with how we communicate in the

"Real World". When we communicate in the "Real World", we have the advantage of using all of our senses to interpret the true meaning of the message being sent to us. In the "Digital World" we have vision as our primary (and often only) sense by which to interpret a message. This means that when a message comes across as ambiguous in the "Digital World", we are often left to guess the true meaning. For example, you might receive a message that says "I'm hanging out with my favorite person tonight". The recipient of the message will often go through a checklist in their mind to help determine the true meaning of the message. They may ask themselves "What did that mean?" "Were they being sarcastic?"

Communicating in the "Real World" has layers of complexity. Maybe what is said is the socially acceptable response, but hidden within the message are clues to the sender's true feelings on the matter? Maybe you say something to one of your friends and by their body language and the tone of their voice, you notice a little defensiveness, possibly even a hurt expression comes across their face. This allows for the opportunity to clarify what you meant or even backpedal and apologize. For example, Sarah, a high school student, had a friend say to her "I'd never wear that dress, but it looks good on you." Seeing the hurt look on Sarah's face, the friend immediately clarified that she felt that the color didn't match her complexion. But in the "Digital World" your friend may not pick up on your true feelings, which can leave them feeling insulted. The best way to protect your child from online miscommunications is to warn them about the weaknesses of digital communication and help them identify when a conversation needs to be done face to face.

Despite how bad these digital miscommunications are, they are not the worst byproduct of the "Digital World". The final contrast between the "Real World" and the "Digital World" is by far the largest producer of online strife. In the "Real World", we see our actions as having identity. In other words, there are things we will never do in the "Real World" because we are too embarrassed or we are afraid that people might get the wrong impression of us. But, in the "Digital World", we feel like our actions have anonymity. This perceived anonymity is the source of most of the cruel or rotten behavior which children display online, especially when those actions seem "out of character" or unusual for that child.

A good example of this phenomenon was brought to Don's attention while he was a middle school D.A.R.E. officer. Amy, a

D.A.R.E. student, approached Don with a copy of a post that somebody left on her Myspace page. The post accused Amy of being a slut and hinted that she might be a lesbian. Eventually Amy discovered that her best friend, Emily, had written the post, because she was jealous that Amy made a new friend. Emily admitted that she wrote the post because she thought nobody would find out it came from her. We have witnessed shocking personality changes when children go from the "Real World" to the "Digital World". Tim and Don have both watched as stunned parents read, in black and white, text logs of what their child has written to another student. It's easy to blame impulsiveness and immaturity on the negative things we see children doing when they are in the "Digital World". In fact, we are sure that impulsiveness and immaturity have a role in many of these scenarios. But, we also believe that there are other forces at work, which influence our children in this new medium. We will delve deeper into each of these forces later in the book.

Digital Danger should be on our radar because every kid uses technology.

Well, almost every kid.

According to report from the Pew Research Center

- 95% of teens are active users of the Internet
- 75% own a cell phone, up from 45% in 2004

Want some more statistics about kids and technology?

- 89% of teens go online from home
- 77% of teens go online at school
- 71% go online from friends or relatives house
- 60% go online from a library

What are teens doing online?

- 94% go online to do research for school assignments

- 81% go to websites about movies, TV shows, music groups, or sports star
- 77% go online to get news
- 64% of online teens have created some kind of content online
- 57% have watched a video on a video-sharing site like YouTube or Google Video.
- 55% go online to get information about a college, university or other school that they are thinking about attending.
- 38% have bought something online like books, clothes or music
- 28% have looked online for health, dieting or physical fitness information

How else are teens connecting?

- 71% of teens have a cell phone
- 51% of teens with phones talk to friends daily
- 38% of teens send text messages daily
- 65% of teens use an online social network site
- 43% of SNS users send messages through social networks daily
- 77% of teens have a game console

- 55% of teens have a portable gaming device

Two take- home messages from these statistics:

1. Most kids are online.
2. The two most popular places to access the Internet are home and school, in that order.

Given these two facts of digital life, it seems logical and strategic for parents, guardians, and educators to partner in order to educate students about the use and abuse of technology and monitor and enforce rules governing the safe use of technology.

In many ways the Internet is the Wild West; you are the sheriff maintaining order in town. To maintain order you have to know the technology available to you.

If you need some background information the next several pages will be helpful. If you are very current with technology, jump ahead to Chapter 2.

Technology Available to Youth

The technological advancements, which have taken place in just two decades, seem remarkable. To fully comprehend the power of today's technology, we must first look back to the beginning of the personal computer revolution. The first personal computers sold to the general public were the Macintosh and Commodore computer systems. They had anywhere from 64 Kilobytes to 128 Kilobytes of memory, compared to today's computers which have over 500,000 Kilobytes of available memory. The first personal computers were little more than simple gaming devices and word processors. The graphics were crude and the computers themselves were incredibly bulky. Fast-forward to today and 21st Century youth have an abundance of computing options. Gone are the days of needing either a desktop computer or a dial up router to access the Internet. Today, there are a variety of devices which can connect to the Internet, including:

- Desktop computer
- Laptop computer or tablet
- Smartphone
- IPod

- Gaming console like X-Box, Wii, or Playstation

As you can see, your child could have four or five different devices that can access the Internet. In addition to being portable, many of these options are not typically thought of as having an element of digital danger. Educators and law enforcement have seen an increase in reports involving students being Cyber bullied while using devices such as an iPod or a gaming console. Today's parents must exercise greater vigilance when monitoring their children's online activities.

Popular Online Services

The Internet offers millions of different distractions to everyday life. People can shop, do their banking, conduct research, play games, or even write a book in the privacy of their own homes. But, when your child thinks of the Internet, two words pop into their minds – social network! Online gaming may draw a child's interest, but the most popular online pursuit for most children will be social networking, and for good reason.

Social networking services allow your children to not only keep in touch with their friends, but also allow them to get instant updates on friend's activities and watch drama unfold, in real time.

Social networking services give your child a platform to display their most intimate details of their life with 749 of their closest friends. They can receive lightning fast feedback on their photos, videos, and quotes, by way of the "Like" button, "Thumbs Up" button, and a host of emoticons (those little round faces which display a myriad of emotions and actions).

Forums and Message Boards

The predecessor to 21st Century social networking was message boards and online forums. Message boards and forums are not as widely used today, but some people still stumble upon them when using a search engine to find answers to their problems. These services tend to be highly focused, covering niche topics. Forums and message boards allow users to post individual questions, which are answered by other users. The downside to forums is that anybody can answer the question, whether they are credible or not. During his online research, Don has witnessed incorrect answers to questions involving teen pregnancy, STD's, mental health, and personal relationship issues. In addition, the question asker opens themselves up to harassment and ridicule by "Internet Trolls" (somebody who makes sport of taunting and humiliating online users).

Digital Media Sharing Websites

There are many different digital media sharing platforms on the Internet today. One of the most popular is YouTube. YouTube specializes in sharing videos, which are made and uploaded by their users. YouTube has a strong stance against nudity and attempts to screen out adult themed material from younger users, but some videos can still be hurtful. Other video sites are more permissive, allowing nudity and other sexually explicit content. Videos uploaded by YouTube users range from funny to purposefully humiliating. Don has received complaints about videos involving Sexting, malicious pranks, mocking parodies, and violent fights.

One of the most disturbing trends that surfaced on YouTube and other video hosting websites is the filming and posting of teens fighting. In one instance, a young girl was having an online spat with another girl from her class over; you guessed it, a boy. The instigator lured the other girl to her home, under the pretense of having an amicable conversation about their feud. But, when the girl arrived at the home of the instigator, she found herself surrounded by the instigator and seven of her friends. Two kids stood outside and acted as lookouts. Then, the instigator, surrounded by her five remaining friends, proceeded to verbally attack the girl, confronting her about the online spat. The confrontation turned into arguing then name-calling and eventually physical violence, where the instigator beat the girl until she became unconscious. The whole confrontation was taped by one of the girls and eventually uploaded onto the Internet.

Thankfully, the young girl told somebody about it and law enforcement officials got involved. That uploaded video was later used against the perpetrators in court. Even though YouTube has a zero tolerance policy on this type of content, videos can remain unreported for several hours or even days. The risk of allowing user contributions is that irresponsible people can always add inappropriate content.

Social Networking Services

Social networking services allow their users to create their own personal web page. The user may include personal information, like name, age, gender, body type, education, and personal interests. Users also have to ability to post photographs, videos, blogs and links to other websites. Users also have the ability to make connections with friends across the globe. Unfortunately, the number of friends a person possesses is usually associated with social status, compelling users to collect as many friends as they can. This can sometimes prompt a user to accept friend request from people the do not know in the real world. It is not uncommon for middle school and high school students to have as many as 1,000 friends or more.

The first social networking services came into existence in the late 1990's. One of the first social networking sites was Xanga. Xanga allowed users to connect with friends and classmates on a broad scale. The information posted by the user could be seen by hundreds of friends at the same time. In addition, every time a user's friend updated his or her page, the user would be notified without having to visit each friend's blog. Due to the popularity of this concept, many other companies created their own version of the social networking service. Xanga started in 1999, followed by Friendster in 2002. Then came Myspace in

2003, Facebook in 2004, Twitter in 2006, and Tumblr in 2007. Although similar in concept, each social networking site has its own twist. Myspace caters to music lovers. Friendster evolved into a gaming social network. Tumblr users share photographs, stories, quotes and amusing snippets. Twitter specializes in brief messages and images that capture how you're feeling, what you're doing and where you've been.

Facebook, by far, is the dominant social networking service. Facebook was the first social networking website which required the user to use their real name. Although it is possible to use a fake name on Facebook, it is against their user agreement rules. Facebook uses many different tools to enhance the user's experience. They offer the ability to create common interest groups, such as school campus groups, work groups, and special interest groups. Facebook also gives users many different tools for communications. Users can send notes, instant messages, and receive voice and video calls. In addition, Facebook allows people to "follow" individuals, so that they receive updates about their friends' without having to manually visit a web page. But keep in mind that these tools may allow for a rich user experience, but they reduce your privacy too. That message is the same for all social media services.

A Common Question

Adults often wonder when it is safe for their child to join a social network. This is one of the toughest questions to answer because whether or not you allow your child to join a social network will have consequences. The answer to this question will vary upon the child's age, maturity level, and gender. Perhaps it is better to consider the pros and cons of each decision based upon common arguments cited by parents and children.

First, let's consider the decision to not allow your child to join a social networking service. The negative cited by parents regarding this decision is standing firm against the question "Why can't I join Facebook?" During a training seminar, one parent told Don that she has to defend that decision at least three to four times per week, and this was coming from her 12-year-old daughter. Samantha, the mother of three daughters, sticks by her choice by telling her twelve year old that it is against Facebook's user agreement to join if you are under the age of thirteen. Samantha did later confess that her daughter will be turning thirteen in four months and that she may feel more pressure to allow her daughter to join because she lacked a more compelling argument, other than the age restriction. That statement prompted several parents to chime in and confess that they begrudgingly allowed their child to create a social networking profile because they ran out of counter arguments and energy.

The truth of the matter is that there are many compelling arguments against having a social networking profile and very few reasons to have a social networking profile. One credible argument for joining a social network is that children report feeling like a social outcast if they are not apart of a social network. In fact, 69% of teens ages 12-17 report that people on social networking sites are mostly kind (Pew SNS report Nov. 2011 (Lenhart et al.)

The Downside of a Social Media Profile

However, parents and students also cite many problems with having a social networking profile. The most common concern was online arguments, many of which spill over into the "Real World". The origin of the strife can come from many things. Some students cite online miscommunications, while others blame "Real World" feuds, which evolve into online abuse. According to a Pew Research Survey conducted in 2011, 20% of teen social media users report that people are mostly unkind to them. Here is a list of issues that teens directly attribute to social media.

- 25% of teens report having a social media experience which resulted in an argument.
- 22% experienced an event which ended a relationship
- 13% stated that social media caused friction with their parents
- 13% reported that social media made them feel nervous to go to school the following day
- 8% of teens report that social media arguments caused a physical fight.
- 6% said that social media had gotten them into trouble at school.

The next most common complaint from both parents and students was that social networking is a huge distraction and time waster. A recent survey conducted by the Pew Research Center noted that 80% of teens are members of a social networking service. More than half of those users report going online several times a day to check their account, make posts, or do a status update. During a recent focus group, one student commented that social networking has become somewhat of an obsession with her and another student felt that his grades have suffered because of his online activities. Finally, the third most common complaint, which affects social network users of all ages, is a feeling of low self-esteem. Many people state that when they are looking at other people's social network pages, they sometimes feel bad about themselves. A study conducted by The Netgirls Project and Dr. Amy Slater found that the more girls used the Internet and social media, the more likely they were to have low self-esteem and body image issues. In some cases, people compare their photos with the photos of their associates. While others report getting their feelings hurt when someone "Unfriends" them or ignores their friend request. Students from a focus group noticed that their friends seem to have more fun activities happening in their lives. One student commented that when she looked at her friend's Facebook pages, it appeared as if there was significantly more activity and comments on their pages, in comparison to hers. This prompted another student to comment, "Facebook is like anything else, you get out of it what you put into it." In other words, if you don't interact with others, they are less inclined to comment on your page.

So, whether it's somebody posting something about you or somebody ignoring you, having your feelings hurt while using a social media service is a distinct possibility, just like social interactions in the real world. It's just something to keep in the back of your mind before allowing your child to use an online social media service.

Services Created for Smartphones

Chances are pretty good that if your child is over the age of 12, they have a cell phone. According to a survey conducted by the Pew Research Center, 77% of teens ages 12-17 have a mobile phone. And if your child has a Mobile phone, there is a good possibility that if they don't have a smartphone; they will soon ask you for one. At one time, it was enough to just have a mobile telephone, but times have changed. The smartphone is the new "must have" gadget, with a surprising 31% of teens ages

14-17 owning one. Functioning as both a phone and a computer, it's easy to see the appeal of a smartphone.

The World of Apps

In addition to being handy, smartphones can also be customized. You can choose from hundreds of thousands of applications, or apps, to add to your smartphone, making it as unique as your personality. Some apps are purely for fun: novelty ringtones sounds which certain motions can trigger, and even some of the most addictive video games ever created. Many of these novelty apps are free of charge, but not every app is free. Most applications that charge you a fee are nominal in price, averaging about $1.00. But, these small additions to your smartphone can cost you over time. One parent told Don that her son spent over $150.00 in applications in just one month, most of them games.

Not all applications are benign. Some take on an x-rated tone, like the application, which acts like a scratch off lottery ticket. However, instead of revealing a winning jackpot, it reveals a scantily clad woman. Just keep in mind, the smartphone you give to your child may not resemble the same phone after he or she is done customizing it.

The one thing that adapts well to a smartphone is online social media. It seems like everybody is using their smartphone to connect to Facebook, Twitter, and other social networking services. This allows the user to check up on their friends, even on the go. This is something many of the social media services are capitalizing upon. Social media services like Foursquare, use the geolocation abilities of your smartphone to allow your friends to track where you are, at all times. Other services, like Instagram, allow you to place a geolocation tag to the photos you post on sites like Twitter. Other applications essentially turn your smartphone into a beacon, so that others may find you. If you thought there was too little anonymity in the digital world before, these advanced smartphone apps take it to a whole new level. We can't stress this enough, the smartphone you give to your child can be customized in a way that you never intended. Your child may not know the full capabilities of the applications they choose to add to their phone. Take the time to review the additions your child has made to their phone. Better yet, make a rule that before anything is added to the phone, you must approve it first. It just makes good sense.

Action Step

Get a picture of your child's digital activity.

- How much time do they spend on digital devices?
- What time of day do they use these devices?
- What devices do they use?
- With whom are they communicating via digital devices?

Chapter Two
Assessing Risk in Your Home

Assessing Risky Behaviors

The first step in assessing your risk is to identify what habits or behaviors place you at an elevated threat level. Technology, like any tool can be used safely as long as it is used appropriately. How and where you use technology can significantly affect the threat it poses to your safety. For example, texting while sitting on a couch is safe, but texting behind the wheel of a car increases the threat level significantly. Most of us can understand that unsafe behaviors put us at greater risk but some parents have a hard time prioritizing the behaviors, which pose the greatest threat. The news media highlights several issues, like Internet predators, sexting, and cyberbullying. Aside from the three mentioned above, here is a quick list of concerns, which should be on every parent's radar.

- Online privacy
- Digital reputation, otherwise known as your digital footprint
- Exposure to inappropriate content
- Unethical behavior

First, let's discuss online privacy, which tops the list of parental concerns. Most teens realize that privacy is important, however they don't realize from whom they should hide their personal information. In fact, during a high school focus group, we learned most students felt they were hiding their personal information from their peers. Privacy from their peers is important but they were forgetting about other online entities, which also try to look into their personal information. Teens quickly forget that there are strangers on the Internet. Strangers will try to befriend teens for many reasons; the one that concerns us the most is image mining. There are groups of people who collect and trade images of teens, which are stolen from their social networking profiles. Some of these stolen images are kept in their personal collection while others are placed on adult websites that cater to pedophiles. In order to prevent this, it is best to only friend people you know in the real world.

The next issue of greatest to parents is their child's digital footprint. A digital footprint is the reputation you build through the images and written information you post. A perfect example of a digital footprint is the information a web search uncovers about your child. For instance, if a quick search reveals numerous images and statements of excessive alcohol use, somebody might jump to the conclusion that your child abuses alcohol. We will have a more in-depth discussion about your child's digital footprint later in this chapter.

Quite possibly the oldest complaint about the Internet is the easy access to inappropriate material. An abundance of profanity, pornography, and violence can be found on the Internet. Relatively few websites attempt to verify the age of the user accessing the information. The most common prevention measure taken by parents is to utilize the parental controls for the home computer and mobile phone. For more information on strategies to combat inappropriate content and more, skip to chapter five.

The final concern is that kids display problem behaviors on the Internet that they would not engage in elsewhere. Beginning in the 1990's, we began noticing that student would apply a sliding scale of ethical behavior to their digital world interactions. "The rules of fair play do not apply to the Internet" mindset seems to go beyond social interactions. Take for example the crime of theft. In the real world, most teens wouldn't consider stealing from somebody, yet many illegally download songs. Parents must support and model good online and offline ethical behavior. Otherwise, the argument "Everybody else is doing it" will win.

Unsafe Environments

Spotting unsafe environments in the real world is much easier than identifying them in the digital world. Some websites seem safe on the surface but may play host to viruses and malware designed to attack your computer. Security technology company McAfee commissioned a 2010 study which showed that over one quarter of teens had accidentally allowed their home computer to be infected with a virus or other malware. Viruses and malware are not the only things to be concerned about when you send your child into the digital world. The two greatest risks to your child do not come in the form of a virus, rather they come from online content and human interaction. When parents think of harmful online content, x-rated material immediately comes to mind, but written content may be most damaging. Misinformation, tutorials on how to build dangerous ordnance, or hate speech are examples of digital danger on the Internet. Teens can be impressionable and gullible; they often don't question what they read on the Internet. This makes knowing their online habits so important.

Perhaps the greatest danger on the Internet is the human element, the social interactions between friends and strangers alike. Any website, which allows for a dialog to take place, has the potential to be harmful to your child. Even gaming consoles can be used for two-way communication.

We want to emphasize our point that the Internet can be a dangerous place to send your child without any adult supervision. No software can replace your watchful eye especially when it is accompanied by a good example and plenty of dialogue.

Reporting Incidents, Why It Rarely Happens

It is not uncommon for teens to keep a negative online experience a secret, especially when it involves something embarrassing. During a recent focus group, teens revealed five reasons why they remain silent about online abuse.

- Embarrassment
- Fear that their parents will restrict access to the Internet
- The belief that their parents won't know how to help
- Afraid that if they say something, other will join in on the abuse
- It's no big deal, that's what happens on the Internet

The best thing for a parent to do is be accessible to their child. But, even if you are parent of the year, some topics may still be hard for your teen to discuss with you. They need a few adults with whom they can discuss their issue in a safe, comfortable environment. We suggest identifying three adults to whom they can go to for advice. It can be any three adults you trust. They could be a coach, family member, teacher, neighbor, or their best friend's parent. Your child needs to be aware that some problems are too big to handle alone, and even with the help of an adult, parents or authorities may have to get involved. Having other trusted adults choices will provide your child with a little extra support. The search institute cites having a mentor in your child's life as a youth asset.

Analyzing Your Digital Footprint and How to Improve It

If your child uses the Internet, they probably have a digital footprint. Think of a digital footprint as your child's online reputation or what others can learn about them from the digital world. The information can come from things your child posts, or it can come from their friend's online activity. Places like Facebook, Myspace, Twitter, Instagram and YouTube curate your teen's activity in an easy to browse format. More information about your child can be found in online forums, fan pages, and even their school's webpage. Although the Children's Online Privacy Protection Act or COPPA does protect the online identities of children under the age of 13, very few protections exist for older children.

Curious about your child's digital footprint? Try doing an Internet search using a search engine such as Google to see what you discover. Then ask yourself, what kind of impression does that information give you about your child? A recent Pew Research Survey found that the older a child is, the more discriminating they are about what they post online.

Approximately 67% of 17 year olds withheld online content, for fear of damaging their online reputation, 30% higher than those polled who were less than 14 years of age. Older teens realize that their online reputation could affect where they go to school or where they will be hired to work. Unfortunately, if they wait till they are 17 years old, it might be too late to repair the damage that has been done to their online reputation. When speaking to teens, we ask them to think about where they would like to be in five years and what skills or traits they must possess to attain their goal. Then, we suggest that they start working on creating a positive digital footprint to help them along their way, remaining aware that the next post that could harm their reputation. A digital footprint that includes positive and diverse experiences can help college admission and job seeking. The sooner you start branding yourself in a positive way, the stronger your digital reputation.

Action Step

Are you curious about your digital footprint? Take a few minutes to run a Google search using your child's name.

Chapter Three
Bullying and Cyber Bullying

What is Bullying?

It is time for us to get on the same page with behaviors loosely defined as "bullying". Bullying has been around a long time. When Tim told his mother that he was collaborating on a book about cyber bullying, she told him this story about the first day of her freshman year in high school.

On the first day of school and occasionally throughout the year, upperclassmen would grab freshman, place them on the drinking fountain and turn on the water. Yearbook photographers were there to document this "event". Cyberbullying is new, but the core of bullying remains.

Bullying occurs when:

- **There is an imbalance of power**

  An imbalance of power can come in many forms. Most of us automatically think of physical size because it is the most visible difference. However, power differentials can also come from inequities in verbal skill, popularity, gender, socioeconomic, and status differences.

- **It happens more than once**

  Many students feel they are bullied every time they get their feelings hurt. But, unless the student is specifically and repeatedly targeted by a peer or a group of peers, it doesn't fit the criteria of bullying used in school systems today.

- **The behavior is intentional**
  Sometimes intent can be a hard thing to prove. As students learn to interact, they test the boundaries of acceptable behavior. Feelings get hurt, especially when it comes to digital communication. Bad behavior, poorly executed jokes, and attempts at using sarcasm can often be mistaken as bullying behaviors.

Let's use Tim's mother's first day of high school as an example.

- Was there an imbalance of power?
  - *Yes. The seniors were older, bigger and had status. It was intimidating to the younger students who were placed on the fountain as well as those who watched it.*

- Did it happen more than once?
  - *Yes. The behavior was repeated during the day, often targeting the same students. They also continued this behavior from time to time during the academic year.*

- Was this intentional?
    - *Yes. Planning was involved, as the photographers were ready to record the event.*

A definition of bullying that makes sense to us.

- *Bullying occurs when purposeful acts of meanness are repeated over time in a situation where there is an imbalance of power.*

Back in the day, kids were placed on drinking fountains and the event was recorded in a yearbook that was available one year later.

Today, technology ramps up the impact of bullying. The pictures and videos can be posted immediately to a large audience on Facebook or YouTube. Others can easily access the event over and over again.

Read on to learn more about how cyberbullying has upped the ante.

What is Cyberbullying?

Cyberbullying is one way that kids bully. It can be defined as intentional, online harassment repeated over time in which there is an imbalance of power.

Lets put this definition to the test by applying it to a common occurrence, one student regularly posting derogatory comments about another student. In this case, Jill posts comments critiquing the outfits that Jane is wearing to school.

- Was there an imbalance of power?
    - *Yes. Jane cannot stop Jill from posting derogatory comments. Jill now has numbers on her side, she has an audience following, and enjoying, the posts.*

- Did it happen more than once?
    - *Yes. The derogatory posts continued for several months.*

- Was this intentional?
    - *Yes. Jill knew that the posts would upset Jane.*

What Strategies Do Cyberbullies Use?

Cyberbullies use e-mail, cell phone text messaging, instant messaging, and various forms of technological communication (Willard, 2006).

They harass, stalk, defame, impersonate.

Http://www.stopcyberbullying.org describes other ways kids may cyberbully other kids.

Kids may:

- Send hateful or threatening messages to other kids.

- Blog to damage other kids' reputations or invade their privacy. For example, in one case, a boy posted a bunch of blogs about his breakup with his ex-girlfriend, explaining how she destroyed his life, calling her degrading names.

- Post other kids' personal information and pictures, which put those people at a greater risk of being contacted or found by strangers.

- Send mass emails to other users that include nude or degrading pictures of others.

- Create internet polls that "rate" others including questions such as
    - Who's Hot?
    - Who's Not?
    - Who is the Biggest Slut in the Sixth Grade?
    - Rate Your Teacher!

- Verbally abuse others during online interactive gaming

Sounds awful, doesn't it?
Trust us, it is.

How Prevalent is Cyberbullying?

Kids have bullied each other for a long time; the game-changers are the digital weapons that bullies add to their toolkit.

The question

- How often are students victims of cyberbullying?

The answer

- Depends on the study.

Most credible statistics range from 9% (Kessell, Schneider et.al (2012) to 50% (bullying statistics.org).
9% - 50% is a big range, why the gap?

The differences in reported rates of cyberbullying are attributed to the way the questions are asked and how cyberbullying is defined. The looser the definition of cyberbullying, the higher the reported rate, the tighter the definition of cyberbullying the lower the rate.

Even the lowest estimate reflects a significant number of students. Besides, if you know that only one kid is impacted, (and that kid is your child) one cyberbullying victim is too many.

Impact of Cyberbullying

So what's the big deal?

> *Kids bully other kids; it's a rite of passage.*
> *No one really gets hurt, do they?*

Think again. We have listened to victims of cyberbullying tell their stories, heard the pain, hurt, and sense of helplessness. The impact can be dramatic. Some may withdraw from school activities, and become ill, depressed, or suicidal (Willard, 2006a).

We all agree on one point, no one wants his or her kid to go through that kind of pain. Life is tough enough for kids as they attempt to define who they are and what they are about. Add in cyberbullying and it becomes the tipping point for some kids.

Shouldn't we do all that we can to stand in the way of cyberbullies?

The obvious answer is "Yes, we should do all that we can." The difficulty lies in tackling this task.

Challenges of Addressing Cyberbullying

Cyberbullying is different from face to face bullying in at least one very important way. Electronic communications allow cyber perpetrators to both remain anonymous and high profile. Cyberbullies can send their cyberbullying messages to a large audience while hiding behind their electronic device.

It is tough to get in the way of cyberbullies for several reasons.

- Cyber perpetrators do not feel responsible for the impact of their behavior because they do not see the victim's distress. They can spew their messages without seeing the fallout from their behavior.

- Cyber perpetrators feel that they will not be caught.

- Cyber perpetrators feel safe, protected by technology.

- Cyber perpetrators are empowered to harass students who may not be vulnerable for face-to-face bullying. They can send messages that they would never say in person. This perception of power can be intoxicating to those who are disempowered during face-to-face encounters.

- Cyber bullying can be immediate. No more waiting until you see someone in person to bully them.

- Perpetrators are familiar with, and have access to, technology. This gives them confidence.

When Can Schools Get Involved?

Most states now have legislation in place that requires schools to address electronic harassment in their anti-bullying policies. For example, Ohio House Bill 116 (also known as the "Jessica Logan Act") is in memory of a student who committed suicide due to bullying via texting. This bill expands the scope of Ohio's current anti-bullying law to prohibit harassment by electronic means. This includes harassment, intimidation, and bullying through computers, cell phones, or other electronic devices. The law requires school districts to amend their anti-bullying policies and procedures. Schools can become involved when they suspect that a student is bullied.

What Are The Difficulties When Addressing Cyberbullying in Schools?

Researchers Slonje and Smith (2008) identified three significant challenges faced by schools as they address cyberbullying.

1. Social network and digital devices are popular, making it nearly impossible for many to escape messages. "Don't go online" is advice that kids will not often follow.

2. Cyberbullying is witnessed by a large, digitally connected audience, often making it impossible to determine who has received the messages, aside from the intended victim.

3. The anonymity among cyberbullies adds to the complexity of defining and implementing a successful prevention plan. We can clearly see the fallout but not the perpetrator.

4. Schools struggle to identify the proper roles to assume in allocating preventative measures. Determining who has

the expertise, and available time, to do the work of prevention is a challenge.

Strategies for Schools

With all of these challenges, what can the schools do to stop cyberbullying?

Resarchers Couvillen and Ilieva (2011) propose several strategies to prevent cyberbullying.

- Clearly define and require compliance with the Internet use policies for students. Many schools require students to read and sign an Acceptable Use of School Technology Form.

- Enforce rules and clearly communicate commitment to everyone's digital safety. Kids know when we are serious about enforcing the rules. Schools should post acceptable use of technology rules in language that kids understand.

- Collect data representing the extent of cyberbullying presence among students. This can be accomplished via a student survey. The data can be used to plan prevention and intervention strategies.

- Enforce specific consequences for cyberbullying. Kids are more apt to follow the rules if they know that they will be punished if they violate the rules.
- Consider implementation of a cyberbullying curriculum. Curriculum delivery through collaboration among counselors, health teachers and media specialists has the potential to be successful in the schools. Health teachers have access to students in their classes for wellness-related topics, counselors have skills to intervene with both bullies and victims, and media specialists have knowledge of technology and the Internet.

- Name a faculty or staff member as a trusted person for cyberbullying reporting. It helps to have a point person field concerns and communicate with administration. This eliminates confusion about where to report these incidents.

- Create a response procedure if faculty is approached by

a cyberbullying target or witness. Script a protocol for staff to follow and present that protocol at a staff meeting.

- Provide faculty training on cyberbullying issues. Help faculty understand the negative impact that cyberbullying can have on student attendance and academic performance. Kids who are being bullied may not want to come to school. Even when they are at school they may be focusing on the fear of being bullied, rather than the information that the teacher is presenting.
- Initiate cooperation among the schools, parents, and the community. Consider offering a parent education program on bully prevention. Share information about what the school is doing to prevent and intervene with bullies and cyberbullies. Offer suggestions about roles that parents play in bully prevention.

- Include students in peer-to-peer or school-wide activities. This engages students as collaborators with teachers and administrators. A student-faculty advisory group can plan these activities as well as continue ongoing dialogue on this topic. It is important to model and make the conversations on cyberbullying and its effects ongoing; do not assume that a one-time effort is effective or sufficient.

Before we get to preventing and intervening with cyberbullies in Chapters 5 and 6, our next chapter discusses a challenging digital danger, sexting.

Chapter Four
Sexting

For the record, Don doesn't really like the term "Sexting." Because parents and students bristle when he mentions it. The term makes a frank discussion about this issue impossible because people aren't ready to talk openly about sex. During presentations Don uses the phrase "Sharing Digital Media" in lieu of sexting. It's a broad term, covering movies, images, and texts and it's a way of bringing up the issue of sexting without making people uncomfortable. With that said, let's discuss Sexting, what it is and why people do it.

A Brief History of Sexting

Let's start with the most widely accepted definition of Sexting. Sexting is defined as "The act of sending sexually explicit messages or images, primarily between mobile phones." The concept of sharing sexually explicit material is nothing new. It is simply the mode of transmitting explicit images that has changed over time. This evolution is made clear through a story shared with us by a veteran educator. It was the 1970's and a young woman used a Polaroid Camera to take inappropriate images of herself to sell to fellow students. The only difference between a digital image and a Polaroid image is the speed at which a digital image can multiply and spread. Where a Polaroid image will remain one image, a digital image can multiply to hundreds or even thousands within a short amount of time.

Even though the sexting media craze peaked in the early 21st century, sexting has been around since the late 1990's. In the beginning, sexting was the transmission of sexually explicit text messages, chats, or emails. Don remembers being inundated with copies of sexually explicit chats from concerned parents who didn't know how to begin processing this new threat. Everyone was convinced that this problem couldn't get any worse. Unfortunately, it got worse. As technology improved, Sexting evolved, to include sexually explicit photos and eventually videos. Whether it is an explicit text, a racy photo, or a lewd video, students who share this type of content are risking emotional, social, and even criminal consequences.

Who is Sexting?

Every parent wants to know the answer to the burning question, "Has my child ever sent somebody an inappropriate image?" Some parents turn to the latest study or survey to find the answer. We have provided some information for those who want to know if they should even be concerned about sexting. A recent study conducted by MTV and The Associated Press, uncovered these interesting facts.

- 33% of people age 14-24 have sent a "sext" message
- 15% of people age 14-24 have sent a naked photo to somebody
- Almost 50% of those who shared a naked photo, felt pressured to do so

The MTV/Associated Press study is just one of many on the topic of digital safety. While each survey may record slightly different findings on sexting, they all reflect one commonality. The older a child is, the more likely they are to send somebody an inappropriate image. But, when does this behavior start?

At What Age Should I Be Concerned About Sexting?

One of the most shocking statistics we can share with parents is the age at which children start sharing inappropriate images and texts. Most parents guess that by the end of middle school, their child will be asked to share an inappropriate image with another child. The fact is we should be concerned about this as early as elementary school! Although rare, we have seen cases involving 9-year-old children sending nude or semi-nude images through email or mobile phone. In some cases, they are sending these images to complete strangers. It is much more common for middle school or high school students to share inappropriate images. In fact, 20% of all teenagers have sent nude or semi-nude images of themselves or posted them online. And over 30% of all teenagers have viewed an image, which was originally meant for somebody else (The National Campaign to Prevent Teen and Unplanned Pregnancy and Cosmogirl.com, 2010). Our experience leads us to believe the frequency of inappropriate digital sharing is probably that the statistics show. One of the standard questions we ask when we are speaking to a group of teenagers is "How many of you have seen an inappropriate image, which was not originally intended to be seen by you?" On average, about two thirds of the audience will raise their hand.

So, we suggest that parents consider addressing the issue of Sexting with their children by age 10 and the latest by age 12. After age 12, the chances of their child being solicited for an inappropriate image are very high.

Sexting Friendly Apps and Services

Technology, like any tool, can be used for its intended purpose or it can be adapted for other purposes. In the beginning, sexters used the common mobile phone to send sexually oriented chats to friends and potential suitors. Eventually, mobile phones added a camera function and video, which created a whole new dimension to sexting. Today, new apps and web services exist which make sexting easier and appear safer to users. Most teens understand the risks associated with sharing an inappropriate image. Once the image is sent they lose control over who will see it. The app market has taken advantage of this threat. There are several photo sharing apps, which appear to give the user some control over the photos they send out. The two most popular apps are Snapchat and Facebook's Poke app. Both apps allow the sender to share photos, which disappear after a specified amount of time. Once the recipient opens the photo they will have from 1 second to 10 seconds to view the image before it disappears. This gives the sender some confidence that the image will be seen by the recipient and not shared with unintended people and appears to eliminate the biggest risk associated with sexting. But, it is still possible for the recipient to capture the image by either taking a screenshot of the image or by using a digital camera to take a photo of the mobile phone. It should be noted that if somebody does take a screenshot of your image, both Snapchat and Poke would give you an alert message. While phone apps concentrate on sending images, web services primarily offer web chat and streaming video options. Originally, the web service Stickam catered to performances and seminars, which allowed users to charge viewers a fee to access to their live feeds. It didn't take long for users to adapt this service for use in sexual performances. For a fee, the performer would allow the viewer access to their live feed and even give them the ability to direct the performance. But, is Stickan commonly used by teens? The answer is yes, according to a 2008 Nielsen survey, Stickan was rated the number one online video destination for children ages 12 to 17.

Another web service, Chaturbate, seems to cater specifically to sexually oriented performances. Chaturbate, a portmanteau of chats and masturbate, was launched in 2011 and has gained popularity among web surfers across the globe. Like it or not, this is just a glimpse of the darker side of the Internet and what is readily available to your children. Keeping your children safe in the digital world requires you to be a well-informed and involved parent. You will find chapter 5 to be a useful tool in this fight.

Help, My Child Shared An Inappropriate Photo!

First, although it is shocking, your child isn't the first person to share an inappropriate photo or video. He or she will not be the last. Whether your child sent an image to a friend or had an image stolen from an online album, retrieving all of the images may not be possible. In the digital world, one image can become hundreds in a matter of minutes. Take the case of Suzie, a 14 year old girl who uploaded several provocative images to the photo processing website Photobucket. The images were of the teen dressed in revealing clothing, swimwear, and lingerie. Her intention was to share these photos with her boyfriend, however somebody hacked into her account and shared her pictures with the World Wide Web. The theft happened in 2007 and by 2011 a Google search turned up over 600,000 items highlighting Suzie. One year later, almost 1,000,000 results feature Suzie. She went directly to her parents, who took swift action and contacted the websites who hosted the images. Some sites removed her images while others were less than cooperative. Since the images were not illegal, considered child erotica instead of child pornography, Suzie's family had little recourse. As a result, she lost all control of her images and five years later, they are freely traded among picture collectors in the seediest corners of the Internet. A secondary consequence of the leaked photos was the bullying that took place. Suzie suffered attacks from peers and Internet trolls alike. The attacks ranged from name calling, like branding her a slut, to vicious rumors claiming that Suzie orchestrated the whole event to propel herself to Internet stardom. The incident involving Suzie, albeit extreme, is a possible fate for any child who snaps a racy picture of themselves. An inappropriate photo is like a secret, no matter how private you attempt to keep it somebody always finds it. Unfortunately, preventing the multiplication of the image is not your only concern. One can hardly write a book discussing sexting without including a chapter on cyberbullying, since the two go hand in hand. As we saw in Suzie's case, cyberbullying is an inevitable byproduct of a leaked Sexting image. Name-calling, rumors and speculations, and even physical violence can be some of the consequences of a shared image.

If the ramifications of sending explicit images are so great, why do teens engage in sexting?

Teens are known for behaving impulsively, inappropriately and provocatively are not new. The game changer is that teens have access to technology and they know how to use it. A teen's impulsive decision to snap an inappropriate photo can take on a life of its own. We know that adolescent impulsivity and technology is a risky mix. We also know that technology means that we are losing control of our teens in this part of their life. We want to help, to make sure that our kids don't make mistakes that they cannot unwind.

University of Pennsylvania Doctoral Student, Nora Draper, has studied the reaction of media to adolescent sexting. In her scholarly article, "Is Your Teen at Risk? Discourses of Adolescent Sexting in United States Television News", Ms Draper brings the sharp eye of the academic to the sexting phenomenon.

We should not be surprised by teen's use of cellular technology. Ms Draper reminds us of the unique relationship between teens and their cell phones. Communication is essential to teen identity. The type of phone they have, the color, cover and use of that technology signals part of their identity. Teens can form intense relationships with peers via cell.

Cell phones play an important part in forming and maintaining romantic relationships as they allow teens to stay in constant connection. Teens no longer have to be physically present to communicate; they can stay connected by texting even when only one, not both, is available. (Draper, 2012).

Nor should we be surprised by our impulse to take charge. Media messages are powerful; Ms Draper points out that the media message is that parents and educators are the guardians of teen safety. If the teen is caught sexting, the media message is often, "Where were the parents? What is the school doing about this?"

The message from our society is equally strong as harsh punishments are often delivered to those who engage in sexting. Ms Draper echoes our concerns about sexting by stating, "Considering the potential loss of control over something as powerful as a sexually explicit image, sexting should be viewed as a potentially risky behavior."

We know that there is risk involved in this behavior; the challenge is that cell phones offer positives as well. They allow teens independence from parents (except for paying the cell phone bill) and constant connections with their peers that form relationships.

Education about the very real harm that can befall teens from their risky sexting behaviors is needed. Information from credible sources about the risks and harm of sexting can better equip teens to make responsible choices about their cell phone behaviors.

The Aftermath of a Shared Image

Before we depart from the subject of Sexting, we should cover what to expect when an image of your child is shared with the whole school. During the course of a school year, your local school district could have as many as a dozen or more Sexting incidents involving students. Originally, the image could be sent to a steady boyfriend or girlfriend. But, it's just as common for a student to share an unsolicited photo with a perspective boyfriend or girlfriend. Similar to how a peacock displays its feathers to attract the attention of a mate, your child may send out an inappropriate photo in hope of getting a boyfriend or girlfriend. Whatever the scenario, an image was leaked to your child's classmates. The first thing to consider is that your child isn't the only star in this drama; there are many different characters that have a role to play. Let's break down the event and identify the key players in this soap opera, there are three main characters with whom to acquaint you. The first character is, of course, the image creator. In a sexting event, the image creator is the one sharing the photo, for without the photo, there wouldn't be a story to tell. The second most important character is the image recipient. Now, the recipient can develop the plot in one of two directions. They can either keep the photo to themselves or they can share the photo with a friend. For the sake of the plot, lets say the recipient shares the photo with a friend and that friend goes on to share the photo with everyone they know. That is essentially how most sexters lose control of their photo; they misplace their trust with someone who does not respect them or have their best interests in mind.

Every time a person shares a photo, they have to accept the fact that there is a possibility, a good possibility, the photo will not stay private. In most cases, that photo isn't forwarded when the creator and the recipient are still dating. However, if the recipient breaks up with the creator or if the recipient is only a casual acquaintance, then the risk of having that photo go "viral" significantly increases. It is even more likely if the creator breaks up with the recipient. As you can imagine, the social ramifications of having an intimate photo leaked to the masses is great. Although, like most things, it will be the center of focus until the next bit of juicy gossip comes along. One interesting fact to make note of is the social impact to the person forwarding the inappropriate image. The person or people forwarding the image will experience little to no social impact. But social ramifications are not the only concern here; there can be school sanctions and criminal charges too. These sanctions will be imposed upon anybody involved in the sexting event, regardless of the role they played.

Most schools have strict policies against such behavior and they may be required to contact either Children's Services and law enforcement agencies, or both. If law enforcement does get involved, then there could be some very serious criminal charges filed against anybody involved in the incident. If the image includes a minor, anyone under the age of 18, then those who possess the image may be in violation of Child Pornography laws. The Child Pornography laws are written to include anybody who creates, directs, possesses, or distributes any pornographic material involving a minor. If the image involves someone who is under the age of 18 and the image is considered both lewd and lascivious, then you could be charged with Pandering Obscenity Involving a Minor or a similar statute. That means the sender, who created the image, can be charged along with the recipient and anybody else who either received or forwarded the image. When we deliver that message to an auditorium full of middle school or high school students, the inevitable question is "What do I do if I receive an image that I didn't want?" Our answer is simple; if you receive an unwanted sexually oriented image, do not forward it to anybody!!! In addition to that, we suggest that the student erases the image as soon as they realize what was sent to them. Because, their phone is like a mini computer, there will be a timestamp on every action they make on that phone. So, it is possible for an investigator to tell when they received the image, when they opened the image, whether they forwarded or saved that image to another location, and when the image was deleted.

The best way to avoid prosecution is to delete the image as soon as it is received. We also advise that even though they delete the image, it is still on the hard drive of their phone or computer. Deleting the image only removes the shortcut to where that image is stored; it's the equivalent of ripping out the index to a book. How to find the information might be gone, but the content of the book still remains. Its important to remember that the child pornography laws are strict, and for good reason. If loopholes or exceptions are placed upon the law, it may weaken them. Allowing an exception to the child pornography laws can open the door for the true criminal to manipulate the law and avoid prosecution. Instead, law enforcement and prosecutors rely upon common sense application of the law.

For example, it would be against the law for a boy or girl, who is under the age of eighteen, to take an inappropriate photograph of themselves, even if they do nothing with the image. But, it would be rare indeed for a law enforcement agency to arrest a child for such a situation. Law enforcement and prosecutors have their hands full with the true child pornographers, which habitually trade in illicit images involving prepubescent children. Keep in mind that criminal charges are still possible. The reason why law enforcement uses discretion in teen sexting situations is that child pornography laws fall under sexually oriented offenses. Any child pornography charge can be accompanied by the requirement for the offender to register as a sexually oriented offender, every 180 days for 20 years. In a case where a boyfriend and girlfriend are trading inappropriate images, a lesser charge may fit the circumstances of the case better than a charge, which has a 20-year long consequence.

The best advice you can give your child is never share an inappropriate image with anybody. If they do share an inappropriate image, tell them there is a good chance that it might be shown to other people. Finally, let them know that if they receive an inappropriate image on their phone, the best thing to do is to delete it immediately and never forward that image to anybody.

Considerations for Educators

We want to end this chapter with some special considerations, which apply to all educators. When an inappropriate image is shared on your campus, there are a few important rules you must follow. First of all, treat the device, which holds the image like contraband. Consider it to be on par with an illegal drug. If somebody gives you some white powder and tells you its cocaine, do you need to verify that it is truly cocaine? No. The same rule applies to child pornography. You do not have to verify that it is truly child pornography before you can take the phone. Once you are in possession of the phone, nobody looks at it, except for a law enforcement officer. If you take the phone, access the image and show it to fellow educators to determine the identity of the student, you are distributing child pornography! More importantly, you should never send that image to your cell phone or email to use as evidence. One high school principal did just that; he lost his job and had to justify why he sent child pornography to his work email. Instead, here is a quick checklist to follow if you ever do encounter an illicit image while you are working.

- Confiscate the phone and contact the police

- Do not share the image with anybody
- Do not release the phone to anybody other than the police
- If you are familiar with the type of phone, switch it to "airplane mode"
- Write a statement of how the phone came into your possession and why you think it contains child pornography
- Prepare your staff and the superintendent for questions by the news media

It is important to remember that even if the parents of the accused child ask to see the phone, they should not be allowed. Advise them that the police have been called and if they have any questions, they can direct them to the police division in charge of the case. If the parents of the victim depicted in the illicit image want to see the image for themselves, refer them to the police division as well. Expect everyone who is involved in this incident to be defensive. Both the parents and student will feel the social implications.

One final note regarding the mobile phone. We ask that you place the phone on "airplane mode" for a very good reason. Airplane mode keeps the phone from communicating with the mobile service. This will keep the owner of the phone from being able to access the phone, which can be done remotely. The owner has the ability to access the account and delete items from the phone, without even having the phone in their possession. It would be easy for the owner to access their account and delete the image before the police could examine the phone. If you turn the phone off, it is possible that it would require a password to access the phone, which could create problems for the investigator. For that reason, we ask that you put the phone on airplane mode instead of turning the phone off.

Action Step - Advice For Your Children

According to a survey by the Pew Research Center, the majority of teens say their parents are the most influential force in their lives. Take the opportunity to provide them with helpful advice; chances are good that they'll listen to you. Here are some of our favorite tips for preventing Sexting.

- Tell them to never take an image of themselves that they wouldn't want everyone to see - that includes friends, family, or teachers.

- Once you hit send, you lose control of that image. Remind them that one image can become hundreds or even thousands and you can never get them back.

- If you send an inappropriate image to an underage person, you could face Child Pornography charges and have to register as a sexually oriented offender.

- Report to a trusted adult any nude image you receive and never forward that image to anybody else.

- Consider the consequences of taking an inappropriate image of yourself or anybody else. Consequences may involve criminal charges, school suspension, or public humiliation.

Chapter Five
Prevention: Keeping Your Kids Safe

People can and do get themselves into all sorts of digital danger. As education and law enforcement veterans the number of ways that people find trouble in the digital world does not surprise us. It was part of our job.

To increase your awareness of digital danger, look for reports of these events in your local newspaper. Once you tune in to this, you may find examples of harassment, voyeurism, threats, adults posing as teens, professionals arrested for distributing child pornography. It's rough out there.

Better to prevent a problem than to unwind the fallout that digital danger brings. We would all agree with that wisdom, however several things are working against parents as they attempt to keep kids safe online.
First, our kids are digital natives. They became familiar with technology at an early age. They are comfortable with, and

understand how to use technology. It is an important part of their daily lives and is often the preferred way to communicate with their peers. Kids are also good at hiding risky digital behaviors from their parents.

Conversely, parents are digital immigrants. We were born after the digital revolution. Like most immigrants, technology was foreign to us and we have learned to adapt to this unfamiliar landscape. Parents are often playing "catch up to their kids" when they attempt to set and enforce appropriate technology rules.

In addition, kids' technical skills exceed their judgment. Experts call this asynchronous development; their development is out of sync. Their technical skills outpace their intellectual, physical and emotional development. Why is this problem?
Simple!

Their technical skills get them into danger that they had not anticipated and cannot extricate themselves from. They have a false sense of safety and security about technology because they are so familiar and comfortable with it. Getting past the eye rolling that occurs when we try to warn digital natives about digital danger takes perseverance.

Finally, kids appear to be safe when they are using technology in their home. It is natural to let down our guard when we are home, because we falsely assume that we have shut out danger when we lock the front door. We want to exhale when our kids arrive home. Unfortunately, digital danger makes its way around a securely locked front door. We need to combat our complacency and learn more about technology so that we can set and enforce digital safety rules.

How To Set Digital Safety Rules

1 You set the rule.
2 Kids usually comply.
3 If they break the rules you enforce a consequence each and every time.

Sounds pretty simple, doesn't it? No reason to read any further is there?

Sorry, we wish it were that simple. If we are serious about creating digital safety rules we need to do a bit of homework.

Developmental Considerations

The first thing to consider is the age of your child.
We will set more restrictive rules for an elementary student than a middle school student and different rules for a middle school student than a high school student. We want our kids to become more self-reliant as they grow older; one way to help this process is to have our rules become less restrictive as they age. This may mean that if you have more than one kid in the

house, you will have more than one set of rules to monitor. That's OK, your high school kid can drive to the store to pick up a gallon of milk, but you wouldn't think of tossing your keys to a 3rd grader to run the same errand.

Previous Problems

If your kid has run into digital danger before, your rules will be more restrictive for them than if your kid has not run into problems. A great predictor of future behavior is past behavior. When kids make a mistake, they are demonstrating to you that their grasp of technology exceeds their judgment.

Starting the Conversation

A great way to begin a digital danger conversation is to use age-appropriate fiction. Kids like to read about the characters in the book, and discuss the challenges that the characters are experiencing. Kids find it easier to discuss what the characters are experiencing than to share what they are experiencing in their own life.
It is less threatening because it adds a layer of emotional distance. The character in the book is experiencing digital danger, not your child.

Things are happening to that character rather than to your kid. Great conversations can occur as the child is reading the book. Questions such as:

- "What could that character have done differently?"
- "How could the character solve the problem?"
- "Have you noticed anyone in your school facing these situations?"
- "Have you been in a similar situation?"

Want some works of fiction to start digital danger conversations with your child? We have included a book list in the appendix.
Check it out.

Credible Rules

You can create a great big list of digital danger rules that your kid will not follow and you will not monitor. If you want to create digital rules, and we hope you do, only emphasize those rules that you can systematically monitor and enforce.
Keep it simple by trying this process.

Keep It Simple Rule Setting

Create a list with three columns.

- Column 1 "Have At It"
    - Place in this column a list of all of the digital behaviors that you allow. Many parents place the following in this column:
        - Texting, calling, and emailing friends. Using word processing, PowerPoint, Excel, and the Internet for homework and research, using Facebook for social contacts.
- Column 2 "Don't Like It"
    - Place a list of all digital behaviors that you don't like, but you will allow because it is not risky enough to rock the boat over. Many parents place the following behaviors in Column 2
        - Online gaming, profanity, downloading media
- Column 3 "No Way"

- In this column place a list of all digital behaviors that
    - You consider dangerous
    - You are willing to monitor and enforce each rule violation, not matter what.

  Some behaviors that may be out bounds for your family are:

    - Sexting, chat rooms, teasing, threatening, bullying, harassing, giving out your address and phone number.

Schedule a time to talk with your kids about the digital guidelines. Set an appointment; this sets the appropriate tone of seriousness. Consider having your child use the guidelines as their screensaver for the first month until they have memorized the columns.

Decide ahead of time whether you are willing to negotiate and move digital behaviors from one column to another column. This one is up to you.

Remember the content of the columns will be different depending on your child's developmental level. For example, Facebook, online gaming and profanity may be in the "No Way" column for an elementary age child, but may change columns as the youth matures.

Last but not least, establish the consequences if they break a "No Way" rule. Don't fall for the tendency to use the "You're grounded for life" consequence. This consequence goes over about as well as teaching a pig how to sing. (It annoys the pig and makes you look silly.) Set rules that have some weight and that you can monitor. An easy way to do this is to temporarily move some items from your "Have At It" column to your "No Way" column. More about consequences later in this book.

Monitoring Digital Behaviors

Physical Presence

One great way to get in the way of digital danger is to be physically around the electronic devices while the kids are using them. For many kids, this is a great deterrent, but this in not foolproof.

We show a video in which a 12-year-old girl is chatting online with a 35-year-old man. Her parent is in the background, observing, thinking the child is safe but unaware of the age of the person she is chatting with. Sometimes physical presence is not enough. You may need to digitally monitor or digitally limit the kid's use of technology. Software can be your ally.

Our top Monitoring Software Picks

Choosing the right monitoring software package can seem like a daunting task. But, if you know how you are going to use the software and the age of the child it is going to protect, the decision becomes much easier. For example, you wouldn't want to purchase software, which was created to monitor a business if your intent is to protect your 12-year-old son or daughter. So, knowing how the software can help you with online parenting is essential. Before we get into the capabilities of monitoring software, we would like to discuss the two options you have in implementing this highly effective parenting tool. The first option is to download the software and not tell your child that you are monitoring their online activities. Some parents have an ethical dilemma with secretly "spying" on their child. We don't see the use of monitoring software as "spying"; instead, we see it as an essential parenting tool, which levels a difficult playing field. Parenting is hard enough without adding the hurdle of never really know where your child is going in cyberspace, who he or she is talking to, or how they spend their time online. In the physical world, we keep an eye on where they are going, what they are doing, and whom they are with, yet we don't consider it spying. Monitoring software enables us to bring our online parenting skills in line with our physical world parenting standards. But, if you still feel uncomfortable about placing monitoring software on your computer without notifying your child, then its fine to tell them what you are doing. As you can understand, your child may feel uncomfortable, or even angry with you installing monitoring software. If this happens, let them know you have complete confidence in them; it's the millions of strangers that occupy the Internet that you don't trust.

Let's face facts, the only way you can know exactly what you child is doing in cyberspace is to employ some type of monitoring software. Ideally, you want a software package that can adapt to the changing needs as children age. Initially, website and keyword blocking will be the most useful tool while monitoring younger children. You will usually be nearby when they are on the Internet and those blocking features will prevent them from accidentally stumbling upon an inappropriate website. But as they get older, the more advanced features will give you a better picture of your child's online activities. Here is a list of useful applications you want to have available in your monitoring software package.

- Keystroke logging, so you can see what they are writing.
- Screenshot logging and a record of the websites they've visited.
- A record of recently used applications.
- A transcript of email and text message activity.
- The ability to block categories or keywords and get keyword alerts.
- Scheduled blocking of the users Internet access.
- The ability to receive email alerts and real time monitoring.

Of course, no program is helpful if you have a hard time using the available features. One of the most common complaints we receive from parents comes from difficulties with reviewing the stored files. When the program captures a user's activity it stores the information, either on the hard drive or on the manufacturer's website. If the information is stored on your hard drive, then you have to use that computer to review the files. This can be complicated if your child is the primary user of that computer. Several monitoring programs can email the files but two hours of captured screenshots can fill your inbox quickly. Some packages offer mobile access. This allows you to access the information with a mobile device or computer, whether it's stored on your hard drive or on the manufacturer's website. We reviewed approximately a dozen different monitoring software packages and selected our three top choices.

1. WebWatcher (http://www.webwatchernow.com)- overall the best choice for simplicity, compatibility (Mac and PC), and web-based monitoring.

2. SpyAgent (http://www.spytech-web.com/spyagent.shtml) - A good option. Not as user friendly as WebWatcher and it allows for only limited remote access (only certain features are available for viewing online). * Only available for PC.

3. Spector Pro by Spector Soft (http://www.spectorsoft.com) - An excellent tool and it is compatible with Mac and PC but it stores the files on

the host computer which can make remote viewing more difficult.

Tips From Parents, For Parents

Some of the best prevention tips are learned from parents. We have listened to thousands of parents share their best prevention advice. We have listed some of our favorites.

Freeze!

John had a philosophical problem with downloading monitoring software onto his home computer. Instead, he developed a rule of his own called the **Freeze Policy**. When John wanted to know what his teenage son was doing on the computer, he would walk into the room and say, "Freeze!" His son would take his hands off the keyboard and John would be able to see what was on the screen.

In one case, this rule averted a potential catastrophe. His son was researching how to build a medieval trebuchet so that he could launch a pumpkin over his neighbor's house. The following week, John signed his son up for the high school hosted robotics club.

Know Their Online Friends

Like most busy parents, Catherine found it hard to keep track of her daughter's online activities. So, Catherine decided to put her efforts into learning about her daughter's online friends. Following her daughter's friends online posts, allowed her to learn about her daughter's planned activities. She uncovered plans for a large, un-chaperoned party that her daughter planned to attend. A simple phone call to the host's parents derailed the biggest party of the school year.

Digital Curfew

Anna had a 7th grade daughter. She noticed that her daughter was being harassed by a group of girls when she was using her AOL Instant Messenger account. Anna instructed her daughter to save all of the abusive chat. After reviewing the chats, Anna noticed that most of the abuse occurred after midnight. She placed an Internet curfew on her daughter's activities; the harassment reduced significantly.

Please note the importance of keeping a record of any abusive chats or emails. This will help prove your case to your child's school or to law enforcement if your parent intervention is not successful.

Know Your Child's Online Passwords

This is perhaps the most important strategy of all. Keep all of your child's passwords. David instituted the "No Secret Passwords Rule". His child didn't have a lock on his bedroom door, why should he have a secret password on his email. Once you have the online passwords check their digital communications on a regular basis.

Know the Capabilities of Your Technology

We suggest that you learn:

- How the technology you use works
- How it stores information
- How long that information stays around

At a minimum know how to check:

- History of your computer

- Temporary internet files

- Chats sent from your child's instant messenger account

- In addition, know how to use your child's cell phone. A cell phone is a mini computer, capable of doing just about everything that your home computer can do. If something is awry, chances are you will find the evidence on your child's cell phone first.

- Finally, know how to find information on certain Internet websites. For example, consider what Kari H. discovered from the website MapQuest. Kari found that if you click on the arrow inside the address box, the last few direction requests pop up. For Kari, this technique revealed the address to a local hotel. She checked the credit card statement, which listed a charge for that hotel from two weeks ago, the same date her husband had an overnight business trip. For Kari, this was the key piece of information to prove her husband's infidelity.

Monitoring Software

Parents often hesitate when we suggest using monitoring software on their computers. Many feel that it's an invasion of privacy. Others feel that it would betray their child's trust.

- Consider telling them that you have installed the software because you trust them; you do not trust others using the Internet.
- Other parents choose to keep the software a secret and keep the source of the information they discover a secret.

I'll share this story; there are many others. Sarah noticed that her daughter was becoming withdrawn and "not herself". Her daughter was also texting more than usual. When she would peek her head into her daughter's bedroom, her daughter would hide her activity by minimizing the screen.

When Sarah tried to check the history of her daughter's computer, it was wiped clean. Concerned, Sarah downloaded monitoring software onto her daughter's computer. Within 24 hours of downloading the software, she discovered several sexually oriented chats and a password to her daughter's secret email account.

Sarah accessed the email account and found several emails from a male friend. One of the emails instructed her daughter how to delete the history of the computer's temporary Internet files.

The email further instructed the girl to delete all emails from the sender, which the daughter neglected to do. Sarah immediately contacted the local police division for help.
Sarah's daughter was communicating with was a 37 year old man, who lived about 12 miles away. That man was eventually arrested for transmitting harmful matter to a juvenile.

Educating Yourself

When educating yourself in the realm of digital safety, you will find credible information online as well as offline. Online information can be found on literally hundreds of different websites. Government entities, Non-profits, and private businesses all have great information on Internet and Digital Safety. We have listed some of our favorite websites at the end of this book.

Offline information can come from both anticipated and unexpected sources. Books are a great resource for sound professional advice; since you're reading our book, you are off to a good start.

Most local police divisions have a community relations unit with officers capable of providing you with the most up to date prevention information. But, not all sources of information come from professionals.

Other parents can yield some of the most up to date information. Parents are on the front lines, trying new ideas every day. They can tell you what ideas worked and what has flopped. They can tell you what the latest trends are and how the kids in your area are getting into mischief. Some of the most resourceful suggestions I've heard have come from seasoned parents.

This may come as a surprise, but some really good information comes from the children themselves. Not only are they digital natives but they are both the victims and the perpetrators of the issues you are trying to solve. They can tell about the latest trends, where it is happening, and why kids are doing it. An added bonus is that when you ask your child to teach you, they are more than willing to share information with you. The more you talk with your child about their online activities, the more likely it is that they will tell you when something is wrong.

Vigilance With A Twist

Remember to engage your children. Ask them questions, listen to their stories and share your safety tips. Pretty standard advice isn't it?

Most parents think that their kids won't listen to what you say. The twist, have digital safety conversations that you want your child to overhear.

Kids are sponges; they have the uncanny ability to absorb the words that weren't meant for them. Just have a conversation with your spouse or a friend when your child is within earshot. The conversation should include a story about something that happened to another parent's child and they will be all ears.

Make sure your story includes:

- An activity you want your child to avoid
- The dangers that activity possesses

- How the problem was solved.

One simple story will spotlight the risky activity, why the activity is dangerous, and how to solve the problem. Since they were not the victims of another lecture, they will listen closely.
A resourceful parent shared a good example of this technique in action with us. June, a parent of a 15-year-old boy, recounted an event, which took place in her household. June knew that she had a very bright and curious son. She also knew that he was more knowledgeable about computers than she was and this concerned her greatly. So much, in fact, that she purchased monitoring software for the home computer. June felt that monitoring software was the only way she could level the playing field and allow her the chance to protect her son from online dangers. After a few months, June discovered some questionable chat logs. She found out that her son was communicating with a stranger online. To make matters worse, the two of them had been planning to meet at a local event, which was two weeks away. June felt trapped by the fact that she discovered this information with the help of monitoring software, or what her son called "Spy Software".

Feeling the need to intervene on her son's behalf, but not wanting him to feel betrayed, June looked hard for a solution.

With the help of a good friend, she orchestrated a discussion with her friend, which would take place within earshot of her son. June's friend, Emily, shared a news story she read on the Internet about a boy who befriended someone online and then met the person at a local coffee shop. There the boy discovered the person did not fit the online profile. The two women went on to debate whether or not teens at their high school would ever meet an online stranger. June asked her son what he thought and her son quickly dismissed the notion. June immediately thought their plan had failed. However, two days later, her son was talking to his online friend and called the meeting off. June's son admitted that he was going to meet one of his friends from Myspace. This was the teachable moment June was looking for. They talked for about an hour, discussing the pros and cons of meeting people from the Internet and how people online could pretend to be anybody they wanted to be. With her son's help, June was able to make contact with the other child's mother, who had no idea that her daughter was going to meet an online friend in the "real world". Together, the parents planned a safe, public, and chaperoned meeting. Even though the meeting went well and the kids are still friends today, both parents agreed that meeting strangers from the Internet is not the best practice.

Chapter Six
Intervention

Intervening When Your Child Breaks Digital Rules

The time may come when, despite your best prevention efforts, your kid finds digital danger. Maybe you notice that your kid is breaking your digital curfew. Perhaps your monitoring software has alerted you to an area of concern? Maybe, you discover communication that your teen is planning a rendezvous with a thirty -year -old stranger? Whatever the danger, it is clear that your kid has blown past your rules and it is time to intervene.

Let's get clear about what it means to intervene. Most people confuse intervention with confrontation. They think of an intervention as an aggressive, "Get in their face" encounter. Nor is it a chance to blow off steam and show them "Who is in charge here". Act on this misperception and you are likely to give the best speech that you will later regret.

An intervention works best when it is a dialogue, not a monologue. Your intervention is best heard when your voice is kept at a conversational level.

Your intervention is most impactful when you spotlight the difference between what your child said they were going to do and what they actually did. Then you clearly and calmly state the consequence for breaking that rule. One way to say it is "You agreed to a digital curfew of 11:00, yet I found out that you were online at 1:00 a.m." Set the consequence. "For the next month I will place your digital device in my bedroom when I go to bed, you can have it back each morning." Set a consequence that considers the previous problem behaviors of the child. Avoid the natural, yet ineffective, "No more digital devices for you for the rest of your life." Make sure the consequence is appropriate for the transgression and considers the track record of your child.

A skillful intervention is meant to keep the lines of communication open and replaces risky digital behavior with safer digital behavior, while keeping your authority firmly in place.

Interventions are essential because kids will try to solve the problem themselves, and will often end up making things worse. We wish that kids would remember The First Rule of Holes, but they don't.
"First Rule of Holes: When you find yourself in a hole, stop digging."

Kids may try to go at it alone because they want to avoid consequences for breaking your technology rules and they think that they can clean this up before you find out.
Often, they think that you are not tech savvy enough to help them.

Set aside enough time to talk about the violation of your digital rules in a civil manner. This will amplify the importance of the digital rule and will set the proper tone.

A Special Consideration

No one wants to find out that your child is the aggressor. If you find that your child is a cyberbully, immediate action is needed. Being a cyberbully is not a rite of passage; it is an indicator that more problems are ahead. Many studies indicate the cyberbullies are more apt to drop out and continue to break the law.

Some actions to take when you find out that your kid is a cyberbully.

- Set an appointment to talk with your child.
- Point out the offending behavior so that the child clearly knows which of their behaviors constitute bullying. Sometimes kids do not understand that the behavior is cyberbullying.
- Let your child know that the behavior is wrong.
- Establish a consequence for the behavior.

- Explain that you will enforce the consequence every time that you discover that the child is cyberbullying.

You have now established what you want to child to stop doing. Most parents stop here, however your next step is critical to the success of your intervention.

- Replace the cyberbullying behavior with a positive behavior. This intervention is especially effective if the child will engage in the positive behavior during the time of day in which they previously engaged in cyberbullying. For instance, if the child cyberbullies in the afternoon, suggest joining an after- school club or activity. If they cyberbully in the evening, sign them up for an evening martial arts class. The concept is pretty simple. You want them to stop being a cyberbully and start engaging in more positive behaviors. This approach has been used successfully with many types of behavioral change. People have stopped smoking by starting chewing sugarless gum, stopped drinking alcohol by attending AA meetings, and stopped negative self-talk by thinking more accurate and realistic thoughts about themselves.

Expect some pushback from your child. They are being asked to give up cyberbullying behavior that, from their point of view, is working. This is why it is critical that parents help the child replace cyberbullying with a positive activity that will work for them.

When Your Child is Facing Digital Danger

What are some of the warning signs that your kid may be in digital danger?

- You notice that your kid is sneakier and more secretive about their use of computer, they may try to change screens or switch off the computer when you enter the room.

- There is a change in their mood; they are becoming more sullen around you. They appear to be preoccupied and tense.

- Their interests change. They are more knowledgeable about age- inappropriate events.

- Their friends change; they want to be around an older crowd and attend events that more mature students will attend.
- Their language changes; they use terms that you are unfamiliar with.

- Their grades drop
- They quit activities that they previously enjoyed.
- Teachers and parents may ask, "Is everything OK with your kid?"

You may be asking yourself if these are just indicators of normal adolescent development. However when there is a sudden, dramatic change in any of these areas, it is wise to pay attention. For instance, your kid's grades may drop from year to year simply because they are taking harder courses, however a sudden unexpected grade decline is not normal. While kids may decide to not participate in marching band next year, it is not common to want to drop band next week.

Developing Your Plan of Action

Ongoing communication with your child will increase the opportunities to discuss the specifics of the digital danger. As you learn what your child is facing, you will develop a plan of action.

- Try to get as much specific information from your child as you can.

- What is happening? When is it happening? Who is behind this?

- What has the child done to try to solve this?

- Write down the information that the child is sharing with you. This will be helpful if you are going to report the danger to the school or law enforcement. Also, taking notes shows the child that you are listening and taking this seriously.

- Remember to check your own emotions. Carefully consider your next step. It is easy to get caught up in emotions when your child is under attack. Think through what is in the best interest of your child. Your child needs a both a cool head and strong advocate.

- Remember that your child will have to live day to day with your attempts to help.

- Watch for your own triggers. If this situation pushes your buttons, make sure that you talk it through with someone other than your child. Were you bullied as a child? If so, you will likely overreact or underreact. Neither of these is helpful with the current situation you are facing.

Avoid common parenting traps.

- First, don't teach, "responding in kind". There is an old Chinese proverb that warns us "Don't roll in the mud with pigs, they like it and they are good at it." Cyber bullies like it and they are better at it than your kid. Wanting to punch the cyberbully in the throat is understandable, just don't act on it. Don't teach your kid to bully back.

- Second, don't teach your child to ignore the problem. Grandma's advice to "Just ignore them and they will go away" doesn't work with cyberbullies. A reasonable plan of action, not inaction, is needed.

- Instead, empathize and develop a plan of action. Send a clear message that bullying is wrong. Kids will often feel they are to blame for this situation. Correct that error in their thinking, quickly. Tell the child that this is not their fault. Discuss future action with your child. They are part of the solution, they should help you develop your plan of action

- Reassure the child that you will consult with them before you act. Kids often think that a plan of action will make things worse. Explain to the child that that they will be aware of all that is happening. No surprises.

- Reach out to others to get their perspective on your plan of action. We do not want our kids handling this situation on their own, you should not shoulder this responsibility yourselves either. Bounce the situation around with friends, family members, work associates, church members. You get the idea, many perspectives help.

Providing Consequences When Your Child Breaks Digital Rules

After the intervention, you may need to provide some kind of consequence.

There are two categories of consequences, logical consequences and natural consequences. Natural consequences result from actions of the child and are not imposed by the parent. For instance, your child may not study for a social studies test and may receive a low grade. The natural consequence is the low grade. Logical consequences result from actions of the child; the consequence is logically related to the child's action and is imposed by the parent. Your child may not study for the test, receive a failing grade, you ban after school activities until the child raises the social studies grade.

Logical and natural consequences both influence behavior. For prevention purposes we recommend that you set logical consequences for your child's digital transgressions.

Allowing your child to experience only natural consequences brings unnecessary risk to the child. We advise against relying on natural consequence that results from digital danger. If a child experiences the natural consequence of failing a test, they have the option to make up the low grade. Cyberbullying is different because it is not easy to make up the harm caused by sexting, cyberbullying, or planning a rendezvous with an adult.
Logical consequences seek to prevent the logical consequence from happening again to your child. We need to focus on getting in the way of future harm rather than allowing the child to experience and re-experience the harm that is a natural consequence of their actions.

Tips for setting logical consequences

Time limited

Meaningful consequences are time-limited. Avoid the temptation to "Ground the child for life." Our experience tells us that it is better to set reasonable consequences for a reasonable, age appropriate amount of time. You don't want the consequence to be so long that the child forgets the reason why they are experiencing the consequence.

Monitored

Insure that you can monitor the consequence. If the consequence you set is "No digital devices for a month", make sure that you can monitor digital device use for a month. This teaches the child that you mean what you say.

Logically related to the behavior

Consequences that are logically related to transgressions add clarity to the punishment. Kids may not get the connection if the consequence for violating digital curfew is "No dessert for a month". Compare it with the consequence "No digital media after 6:00 for a month."

Which of these consequences do you think makes more sense to the child?

Phased out

Allow the child to demonstrate compliance with your digital rules before the consequence is totally removed.

For instance, you may have set a consequence "No digital media for a month". After a month, you may want to phase it out with the sanction "You may use digital media this week to demonstrate that you can follow digital rules."

- This sends two messages:
    - I am still monitoring your behavior.
    - Lifting the sanction does not mean that you can wait me out and return to the risky digital behavior that resulted in the original consequence.

A Common Digital Violation

One of the most common digital rules violations occurs when students use digital media after parents have gone to bed. This is risky behavior for several reasons.

Grades may suffer. Students rush through homework to get to their digital media. This encourages kids to communicate with others who are up at that hour. This means that your child is communicating with people older than your child, children who are ignoring their parent's rules or children who have no digital curfew. Ask yourself if this is the type of digital peer group you want your child to experience.

Kids using digital media after bedtime are at risk for disrupted sleep. Pediatricians stress the importance of sleep for growing minds and bodies.

Back in the day, kids would have to physically sneak out of their house to put themselves in some type of jeopardy. Now, with digital media, kids can place themselves in jeopardy by using digital media past their curfew. In a sense they are sneaking out of your house after you are asleep.

A Common Example: Jon and Mike

Jon is like most parents, he wants to trust his teen, Mike. For the most part Mike follows the rules at home and at school. Late one night, Jon has trouble sleeping, hears some activity in Mike's room. Investigating, he learns that Mike is on Facebook conversing with "friends".
Jon Takes These Steps

- Sets a time to talk the next day.
- Keeps his cool during the talk.

- Sets the consequence that Mike may not use digital devices after 6:00 p.m.
- Listens to Mike's objections and stands his ground.
- Monitors the consequence every evening.
- After a month of compliance, Jon sets the digital device curfew at 9:00 p.m. and monitors compliance for a week.
- After one week of monitoring the phased out consequences, Jon sets the digital device curfew at 11:00 p.m.

Can you see yourself intervening and sticking to the consequences that you set? If not, you may want to seek the support of others who can help you through this process. A few sources of support:

- Teachers
- Coaches
- School Counselors
- Youth ministers
- Pastors
- School Resource Officers
- Neighbors
- Friends who have the same age child

Action Step

Try out an intervention with this scenario. You discover that your child is frequently using social media past midnight on school nights.

- What type of consequence would you set?
- How would you enforce it?
- What resistance would you expect?

Chapter Seven
Legal Issues

Willfully Breaking the Law

We speak with thousands of students every year about cyber bullying, sexting, digital safety, and maintaining a healthy digital footprint. We are often met with an auditorium of stunned faces when telling the students that something they do online could be against the law. Because of the nature of the Internet, students find it hard to see that actions they take online do have consequences. The way we experience life in the real world is much different than how we experience things online. So, educating students on the laws covering our online actions is usually an eye opening experience. Students can see how threatening someone, breaking into their home, playing a mean prank on someone, or stealing from somebody is a crime.

However, when we apply similar crimes to the Internet, students want to argue against criminal charges. So, if you threaten somebody online, students argue that you shouldn't get arrested because you couldn't possibly harm them through the Internet.

If you hack into their Facebook account and post something extremely embarrassing about them, it's just a gag and there is no real harm. And the most strongly debated case, if you download a song for free from the Internet, it's not really stealing because you can't hold it; students think it's not real property. Perhaps it's because of the third person way we experience the Internet that children fail to see that their actions result in real consequences and in some cases, criminal charges. Also interesting to note is that the most common precipitant that results in criminal charges stems from impulsivity. Angry with somebody? How about hacking into their Facebook account and trash their reputation? However, accessing somebody's online account without his or her permission is a crime. In fact, hacking into any account or accessing their computer without their permission is against the law. Kids have a hard time understanding this concept. What if the Bully has your cell number? A more direct approach would be for the bully to send a text threatening to beat up another kid. Menacing, whether in person or through a cell phone is a crime, as long as somebody believes you have the capability to carry out the threat. Kids are shocked to learn this information. Not all crimes are perpetrated by someone who knew their actions crossed a legal boundary. Some concepts are too abstract for a juvenile to comprehend.

Unintentionally Breaking the Law

There are some other situations where a student finds themselves in trouble and they really can't understand why. They may feel that they have crossed an ethical boundary but truly don't believe they broke any laws. The easiest example to illustrate is Sexting. With Sexting, kids often know that they shouldn't be sharing inappropriate images or videos but believe that because the participants are of the same age, the elements of the event don't rise to a criminal level. This mindset not only allows them to feel comfortable sharing inappropriate images or videos with a boyfriend/girlfriend, but they also view these files as sharable material. The fact is, very few of these traded images remain private. Often, they are shared publicly, with alarming speed and the person in the image is almost always seen as the instigator.

We have been educating students on the laws regarding Sexting for over five years and over the course of those five years, the crowd's reaction is always the same. We advise the students that if you share a photo of someone under the age of 18, where the picture is lewd and lascivious, you are violating a Federal Law.

Which at that point, we see about every third person in the auditorium grab their cell phone and furiously start deleting files. About that time, our Tech guy launches in on his speech on how hard it is to remove a file and that deleting a file doesn't get rid of it. Far from it! We explain to them how effective our local ICAC (Internet Crimes Against Children Task Force) Agents are at retrieving data and their only protection is to delete a questionable file as soon as they receive it. Deleting the file immediately is the defense of a reasonable person. This is the point where students finally start realizing that their online actions do come with real consequences.

Ethical Behavior

Ethical behavior has always been a huge hurdle when dealing with children and their online activities. Since the beginning of the Internet, there has been a blurred perception of ethical behavior when it comes to online activities. We find that there is a definite sliding scale of ethical behavior between offline and online behavior. While mediating incidents involving good kids;

the first thing the parent says is "Not my child!" Unfortunately, even the best children fall prey to this type of behavior. There are several reasons why this may happen. It could be the way children view online culture. I hear statements like "That's just what happens on the Internet." or "It's not like she said it to my face." Viewpoints like that reduce the likelihood of a victim reporting an incident and don't allow the victim to feel justified in feeling hurt or upset. About one in ten victims of cyber bullying will report an incident to a parent or other trusted adult. This limits the child's understanding of acceptable social boundaries. When a child does something inappropriate, the only way they will learn not to repeat the behavior is for somebody to bring it to their attention or to be punished for that action. If nobody reprimands the child, they won't understand that the behavior was inappropriate and the behavior will continue. Of course, a child doesn't have to be reprimanded to learn social boundaries. Often, verbal cues and body language will tip a child off that they've crossed the line. Unfortunately, the only feedback children receive from online communications is the written word. There is a lack of visual and auditory cues that might alert a child when they hurt another person's feelings. They don't see the pained expression or hear the dejected tone. Instead, children appear indifferent, stoic, or even sarcastic to mask the fact that their feelings have been hurt. The concept of ethics in a "make believe digital world" can be a hard one to grasp, even for adults. But the reality is that the "Digital World" is every bit as real as the "Real World". The ethical rules and boundaries we follow in the "Real World" have to be followed in the "Digital World". Our actions in the "Digital World" have impact; things, which hurt in the "Real World", also hurt in the "Digital World". The injuries we sustain online are real and they do affect us in the "Real World".

The First Amendment

Since we are talking about ethical behavior on the Internet and Cyber bullying, we felt it was necessary to discuss the topic of The First Amendment, as it applies to the Internet. The First Amendment does protect speech on the Internet and this can affect when schools and law enforcement can intervene. However, there are four areas of speech, which do not have the protection of the First Amendment.

- Lewd and obscene speech
- Speech that is considered profane
- Libelous speech or false statements about somebody else

- Speech which causes injury or incites violence

Public schools will get involved in a bullying incident if the bullying occurs on school grounds or at a school function. But, in the case of cyberbullying, the incident likely occurred off school grounds and would not be a part of a school function. Even though the Supreme Court has yet to make a decision on the limits of online speech, there have been two lower courts that have weighed in on the topic. In J.S. v. Blue Mountain School District, 650 F.3d 915 (3d Cir. 2011), a middle school student created a fake Myspace page to make fun of her principal. The school suspended the student, which prompted the American Civil Liberties Union to take action on behalf of the student. Eventually, the Third Circuit Court ruled that the spoof Myspace page did not substantially disrupt the school, and the suspension of the student violated her First Amendment rights. Then, in Kowalski v. Berkeley County Schools., 652 F.3d 565 (4th Cir. 2011), a high school student created a Myspace discussion group called SASH (Students Against Sluts Herpes), with the intent of using the discussion group to attack another student. The Fourth Circuit Court determined that the First Amendment did not apply because the student's speech disrupted the victim's ability to learn at school. Both cases had students who created Myspace pages on their own time and in the privacy of their own homes and involved an attack upon a member of the school community. One case was an infringement of the First Amendment and the other was not, but why? Was it because one of the victims was an employee of the school or was it the ages of the victims involved? Neither, it had everything to do with the disruption the Myspace page caused within the school environment. In the case involving the principal of the Blue Mountain School District, the school failed to show that there was a substantial disruption within the school environment.

To help determine whether Internet speech is on-campus speech or off-campus speech, consider two factors. First, did the online post create a foreseeable and substantial disruption to the discipline or work environment of the school? For example, the post might promote unruly behavior among the student body or prevent the staff from being able to do their job. The other factor is whether or not the online speech significantly affects the victim's ability to participate in school. These are just two facts to consider, for more examples refer to the following court decisions.

- Tinker v. Des Moines Independent Community School District, 393 U.S. 503 (1969)
- Bethel School District v. Fraser, 478 U.S. 675 (1986)
- Hazelwood School District v. Kuhlmeier, 484 U.S. 260 (1988)
- Morse v. Frederick, 551 U.S. 393 (2007)
- J.S. v. Blue Mountain Sch. Dist., 650 F.3d 915 (3d Cir. 2011)
- Kowalski v. Berkeley County Sch. Dist., 652 F.3d 565 (4th Cir. 2011)

Chapter 8
Caution: Don't Read This Section Alone or After Dark!

We would like to think that we are safe in our home. All of the kids are home. In the evening we lock doors, close windows, make sure that our garage door is closed, turn on security lights, if we have one, we arm our alarm system.

Seems like we are safe and secure, doesn't it?

However, locks, lights and alarms do not stop digital danger. Criminals can find a way to digitally enter our home and place our children at risk. They may be spending time with your child right now and you (and your child) may think that they are chatting with another teen.

In the chapter, we will share information that will be uncomfortable for you to read. By sharing cases of digital danger, we hope that you will be inspired to take the steps necessary to protect your child. The events that we will highlight in this chapter are real but they are not the norm. They fall under the category of the worst-case scenario and are a product of bad decisions and cruel intentions. They are included so we can learn from the mistakes, which were made before us so that we may improve our skills as parents.

Doctor Feelgood

Back in the late 1990's a man created a website and called himself Doctor Feelgood. The site invited children to write to him with their problems and he would help solve them without getting their parents involved. Dr. Feelgood was not a real doctor and had no medical, psychological, or counseling training, yet he used the title of doctor to mislead children into trusting him. Once, a young girl wrote to him with a problem she felt uncomfortable asking her mother about. The reply she received was mildly sexual in nature and unnerved her enough to discuss it with her parents, who immediately reported the incident. The man was confronted and the website was taken down but it was unclear how many other children had contacted him. Preying upon a child's insecurities is a common ploy used by many predators today.

Giving your child a strong support network is a way of reducing their chances of falling into this type of trap. Earlier in the book we suggested that you identify trusted adults with whom your child can confide. We underline that suggestion here. The more trustworthy people children have to confide in, the less likely they will be to turn to strangers for advice.

The Parent Trap

One day Diane noticed her daughter Stacy wasn't acting like herself. She was moping around the house, had no appetite, and seemed agitated when her phone buzzed with a new text message. Concerned, Diane started probing and eventually discovered that Stacy was receiving threatening text messages from her friend Lexie. Confident in the friendship she had with Lexie's mother, Diane decided to call her and the two of them could help resolve the issue. After reviewing the text messages with the other mother, Diane was confident that the fight would be resolved by the weekend. Friday, Diane heard back from the mother who stated that it was Stacy who started the argument and that she expected Diane to encourage her to apologize to Lexie. The conversation degraded to the point where parents accused the other of enabling their child's bad behavior. The phone call ended with the families no longer on speaking terms.

You may feel confident in the relationship you have with another parent but when you confront them about a bullying incident, the outcome is rarely what you expect. It is the instinct of most parents to believe their child's side of the story, no matter how dubious their version sounds. We are our child's advocates and it goes against every fiber of our being to question their integrity. When possible, try to enlist the help of a mediator, whether it's a counselor, teacher, or when necessary, law enforcement. It may not always be possible to salvage the relationship, but by putting another person in the role of mediator, it allows you to play the role that suits you best, your child's advocate.

Going From Bad to Worse

Denise knew that her daughter, Carrie, was be bullied at school. Carrie's harassment started online but quickly transitions to the classroom after she reported her bully to the Internet service provider for misconduct. When Carrie was bullied in the classroom, Denise reported the misconduct to the school. When the school investigated the incident, the bully had several friends identify Carrie as the instigator. Since nobody came forward on Carrie's behalf, the bully did not receive a punishment. One month later, the online bullying resumed; Denise filed a police report to document the incident. Criminal charges were filed against the bully and the case was brought before the Juvenile Court. This is where the bullying should have stopped, but it didn't. The harassment intensified, several of Carrie's classmates joined in on the abuse, calling her a "snitch". The harassment further escalated prompting Denise to transfer Carrie to another school. In this case, Carrie did just what she was supposed to do. When the harassment started, she told somebody about it. Unfortunately, both parties can appear to be mutual combatants. The victim's attempt at defending themselves may give them the appearance of being a bully too.

A few suggestions for a student who is being harassed on the Internet.

- "Don't fight back."
- Avoid responding to verbal attacks.
- Make sure the child tells the bully to stop contacting them.
- Save every message so that you can document the abuse.

Sextortion

Carolyn enjoyed texting her new Facebook friend, Ryan. He attended a school nearby and like her, was in the marching band. Ryan was attractive, athletic, funny, and patient and best of all, he always had time for her. When she would fight with her Mom, Ryan would say all the right things to make her feel better. Carolyn thought she was the luckiest girl on earth. There was one problem, Ryan wasn't 16 years old, and he was actually 36 years old and lived with his wife and young daughter in a neighboring community. Ryan, an Internet Predator, enjoyed talking to teenage girls; in fact, he had several teenage friends on Facebook who he talked with every day.

But, Ryan had a particular interest in Carolyn and worked hard to find out everything he could about her. Ryan would invest many hours texting Carolyn, gaining her trust and making her feel special. One evening, Ryan convinced Carolyn to take several nude photos of herself and send them to him. That was the last time Carolyn heard from the caring, sweet boy she knew as Ryan. The next time she heard from him, Carolyn couldn't believe it was the same boy. Her stomach tightened as she read the text, "Hey Babe, did you forget about the pics you sent me?

I haven't. Listen carefully, unless you want everybody you know to see the pics you'll do everything I say..." Ryan instructed her to meet him at a nearby park where he picked her up and took her to a local hotel. Ryan demanded that Carolyn have sex with him or he would send her nude photos to everybody she knew. Carolyn agreed to have sex with him three times before her mother discovered one of the text messages and called the police. This case illustrates Grooming, a process, by which a predator gains the trust of a child he or she met on the Internet. Internet Predators have been known to invest as much as two years grooming a child as they attempt to learn everything they can about them. Once they gain the child's trust the predator slowly introduces sexual messages, preying upon the child's natural curiosity. Once the predator thinks they have emotional control over the child, they meet them in the flesh.

We share this case in order to reinforce the need to share the message with your child that an online stranger is just as dangerous as a real world stranger. This will reduce the chance that your child will friend people they do not know.

He Didn't Seem the Type

A special police task force was investigating an Internet user for illegally sharing Child Pornography. After identifying the home belonging to the Internet Protocol address, a search warrant was obtained and the investigators went to speak to the resident. The investigators were met at the door by an elderly couple that appeared quite bewildered by the accusation that they were trading child pornography. Being a minister, the husband hardly fit the profile of a child pornographer; the investigators were beginning to think that somebody else might have found a way to use their online service. The investigators decided to execute the search warrant and conduct a quick sweep of the home; what they found shocked them. The lead detective discovered that the elderly gentleman was in the process of downloading child pornography at that very moment. A forensic search identified thousands of images and videos, which contained child pornography. As the team was loading the evidence into their van they were met by another surprise. A group of parents were waiting outside with their children, asking if they could go inside. The suspect's wife ran a daycare out of their home. The lesson learned by parent and investigator alike was that it is impossible to identify a pedophile by appearance alone. Sometimes, pedophiles and child pornographers are the people we suspect the least. Some of the parents later confessed that the man made them feel uncomfortable but they ignored the feeling because he looked harmless. Parents should always trust their inner voice, just because you can't explain why you feel uncomfortable, doesn't mean the notion is wrong.

Summary

We've covered a lot of ground about the topic of digital danger in this book. Our hope is to empower rather than frighten, to educate rather than overwhelm. We know that most people do not act on the information they receive, they simply learn it, put it away on the shelf, hoping that they never have to take action. We hope you resist that impulse and begin to take action that will prevent digital danger from harming your child.

We offer the following three action steps that will start you down the path toward digital safety. If you do nothing else, at least take these steps.

1 Ask your child to teach you about all digital devices your child uses. Place them in the role of expert, kids love that. This action step allows you to both increase your technical literacy and allows a comfortable starting point for digital danger discussions

2 Take some time to learn how to use the devices; this will help you learn how the device can open the child up to

digital danger. Your child is looking at the digital devices as fun ways to amuse themselves and stay connected with their friends. You view the devices as potentially dangerous. Combining your knowledge from this book with what you have learned from using the digital devices, allows you to move on to step # 3.

3 Create digital rules for your child. Consider outlining your expectations in a Digital Behavior Contract. Educators know that a behavior contract is a great way to keep kids working toward desired behaviors. Contracts clarify what is expected, they add an air of formality. They help kids know that you are serious. Many school districts have rules governing the acceptable use of technology and the Internet. Often they will have students sign a statement that they have read and understand the rules.
Why not create a Digital Behavior Contract for your child. We have provided a sample contract in Appendix IV to get you started.

References

Bullying Statistics retrieved from http://www.bullyingstatistics.org/content/cyber-bullying-statistics.html

Couvillon, M. & Vessela I. (2011). A Review of Schoolwide Preventative Programs and Strategies on Cyberbullying Preventing School Failure, 55(2), 96–101, 2011

Draper, N.R. (2012). Is Your Teen at Risk? Discourses of adolescent sexting in United States television news, Journal of Children and Media, 6:2, 221-236

Kessel, Schneider et al. (2012). Cyberbullying, School Bullying, and Psychological Distress: A Regional Census of High School Students. American Journal of Public Health. Vol 102, No. 1.

The Pew Research Center's Internet & American Life Project 2011 Teen/Parent Survey, April 19 – July 14, 2011.

The Pew Research Center's Teens Smartphone and Texting Study, Amanda Lenhart March 19, 2012.

The Pew Research Center's Parents and Teens Online Privacy Study, Madden et al., November 14, 2012

Adolescent girls who over use Internet and social media suffer lower self-esteem and negative body image. Psychology & Psychiatry July 3, 2012 http://medicalxpress.com/news/2012-07-adolescent-girls-internet-social-media.html#jCp

The National Campaign to Prevent Teen and Unplanned Pregnancy and Cosmogirl.com, "Sex and Tech: Results from a Survey of Teens and Young Adults"; *http://www.thenationalcampaign.org/sextech/PDF/SexTech_Summary.pdf*

Stop Cyberbullying retrieved from http://www.stopcyberbullying.org.

The Secret Online Lives of Teens, Harris Interactive & McAfee, May 4 through May 17 2010

Willard, N. (2006a). Cyberbullying and cyber threats: Responding to the challenge of online social cruelty, threats, and distress. Eugene, OR: Center for Safe and Responsible Internet Use.

Willard, N. (2006b). Flame retardant. School Library Journal, 52(4), 54–56.

Appendix I:
Internet and Digital Safety Websites

http://www.fbi.gov/fun-games/kids/kids-safety

http://www.missingkids.com

http://sheriff.franklincountyohio.gov/safety/internet-safety.cfm

http://www.ohioicac.org/forPARENTS.aspx

http://www.netsmartz.org/safety/safetytips

http://www.isafe.org

Appendix II:
Cyber Dangers Young Adult Book

Upper Arlington Public Library Youth Services Manager Dena Little has compiled a list of fiction for teen readers. With a Master's Degree in Library and Information Science, she knows her stuff.

Anderson, Jodi. *Loser/Queen* (online anonymity) (2010)
Butler, Dori. *The Truth About Truman School* (cyberbullying) (2008)
Davis, Lane. *I Swear* (cyberbullying) (2012)
Finn, Katie. *Top 8* (cyberbullying; hacking) (2008)
Griffith, Adele. *The Julian Game* (online identity) (2010)
Jacobs, Tom. *Teen Cyberbullying Investigated* (Cyberbullying) (2010)
Lange, Erin Jade. *Butter* (cyberbullying) (2012)
Laser, Michael. *Cheater* (cheating using technology) (2008)
Peters, Julie Anne. *By the Time You Read This, I'll be Dead* (cyberbullying) (2010)
Phillips, Suzanne. *Burn: A Novel* (cyberbullying) (2008)

Ruby, Laura. *Bad Apple* (cyberbullying) (2009)

Tanzman, Carol. *Dancergirl* (cyber-stalking) (2011)

Van Tol, Alex. *Viral* (cyberbullying, crime) (2011)

Vaught, Susan. *Going Underground* (cyber-crime) (2011)

Appendix III: Digital Behavior Contract

I agree to abide by the following rules regarding the use of digital devices and the Internet.

1. I will provide all passwords to my parents.
2. I will not use the technology to bully, harass, lie, manipulate, or upset others.
3. I will not participate in chats or posts that hurt others.
4. I will not text or post content that I would not say in person, with my parents in the room.
5. I will not send images of my private parts or others' private parts.
6. I will not access pornography
7. I will not use my devices after 10:00 p.m. on school nights or midnight on weekends.
8. I am financially responsible for replacing any digital devices I damage or lose.

Student Signature ____________________

Made in the USA
Charleston, SC
03 May 2013